Indoor Grilling

TIME-LIFE CUSTOM PUBLISHING

Vice President and Publisher: Terry Newell
Associate Publisher: Teresa Hartnett
Development Editor: Teresa Graham
Vice President of Sales and Marketing: Neil Levin
Director of Special Sales: Liz Ziehl
Managing Editor: Donia Steele
Director of New Product Development: Quentin McAndrew
Production Manager: Carolyn Mills Bounds
Quality Assurance Manager: Miriam P. Newton

Time-Life Books is a division of Time Life Inc.

4 th printing.
Printed in Hong Kong.
TIME-LIFE is a trademark of Time Warner Inc. U.S.A.

Books produced by Time-Life Custom Publishing are available at
special bulk discount for promotional and premium use. Custom
adaptations can also be created to meet your specific marketing goals.
Call 1-800-323-5255.

Library of Congress Cataloging-in-Publication Data

Indoor grilling: great tips and recipes for grilling in the oven and on the stove.
     p.   cm.
     Includes index.
     ISBN 0-7835-0322-9
     1. Barbecue cookery.   I. Time-Life Books.
     TX840.B3154 1997
     641.7'6—dc21   96-38055
                    CIP

Indoor Grilling

**GREAT TIPS AND
RECIPES FOR GRILLING
IN THE OVEN AND
ON THE STOVE**

TIME ®
LIFE
BOOKS

Contents

Introduction

Welcome to the hottest new cooking trend of the '90s! With the abundance of indoor grilling equipment now on the market, you no longer have to wait for balmy weather or the patio of your dreams to enjoy the pleasures of a perfectly charred steak, juicy kababs, or the ultimate burger.

Indoor grilling is a quick, simple, and healthful way to cook, ideal for busy working families who don't have time for elaborate meal preparations. The grills are perfectly suited for gas or electric ranges and ovens. (However, they are not recommended for use on flat—induction or other—stovetops.) You will be surprised to find how easy it is to clean and store the pans and griddles, and they will quickly become an integral part of your kitchen.

This cookbook offers a variety of tasty ways to prepare chicken and steak, as well as fresh ideas for grilling fish and shellfish, lamb, turkey, vegetables, and even fruit. Whether it's a special occasion, such as Garlic-Lemon Shrimp, or everyday fare, such as Dijon Burgers with Grilled Onions, *Indoor Grilling* is there for you.

Indoor grilling equipment comes in two basic models: ridged pans and griddles for stovetop use, and pans fitted with grates to use under your broiler. Both types will successfully create the look and taste of foods cooked over an outdoor fire, and each has unique features. For example, the stovetop pan or griddle allows you to monitor your cooking closely, while the broiler pan encloses your cooking in the oven or broiler, containing spattering.

Be sure to choose a grilling pan or griddle that meets your needs—a small one if you are cooking for one or two, and a large one if you plan to cook large pieces of meat, such as spareribs or whole turkey breasts, or if you need to feed a crowd. You may also prefer to have a roomier model if you want to grill your side dishes along with your main dish. Most of the recipes in this book work best on a large indoor grilling pan or broiler.

STOVETOP GRILLING PANS AND GRIDDLES
Before using your pan or griddle for the first time, wash it by hand using hot soapy water. Rinse and dry your pan or griddle and place it on the stove on top of the burner grates. The elevation provided by the burner grates is necessary for even heating and cooking.

Although your pan or griddle may have a non-stick surface, a light coating of vegetable oil cooking spray or vegetable oil will help to enhance grilling effects. Apply the spray or oil frugally, before preheating. Coating with spray or oil is especially helpful when cooking very lean foods such as skinless chicken, fish, shrimp, turkey, and vegetables. Preheat the oiled grill over low to medium heat only, for just a few minutes. The pan is ready for cooking when water sprinkled on the surface dances and sizzles immediately. Never use medium-high or high heat under your grilling pan or griddle. Extreme heat can become trapped under the pan or griddle and damage your stove.

If you are cooking foods that are quite fatty you may need to drain off drippings occasionally. Before draining, turn off the heat, handle your pan or griddle with potholders, and work over the sink while carefully pouring fat into a heat-proof vessel. Wipe any fat or oil from the sides and bottom of the pan or griddle before returning it to the stove. Never run water on a pan or griddle that is hot, which can cause warping. Never set a hot pan or griddle on a cold surface, which can also cause warping and damage the surface.

When grilling indoors, allow food to cook long enough on each side to scar. Avoid the temptation to turn food over and over, which inhibits browning. The browning is what concentrates flavors and makes grilled food distinctively delicious.

Choose utensils that will preserve and protect your pan or griddle's surface. Preferred utensils are made of nylon or wood. They will not scratch or damage the special surface, and thus will prolong the life of your equipment. Spatulas and tongs are the handiest tools for lifting and turning foods on the grill.

After cooking and cooling, your grilling pan or griddle should never go in the dishwasher. Simply wash it with hot soapy water using a nonabrasive cleaner with a plastic or nylon cleaning pad. Dry thoroughly and you are ready to treat yourself to the next grill recipe.

BROILER GRILLING PANS

Seasoning your broiler grilling pan before you use it the first time will prevent rusting and make the pan much easier to clean, and anything you cook on it will be less likely to stick. To season it, first wash your new pan with hot soapy water and dry it completely. Preheat your oven to 300° F. Rub a thin layer of solid vegetable shortening (never use butter or margarine) over the pan and grate, being sure to cover all corners well. Set the pan in the oven for 1 hour. At the end of that time, set your pan on a heat-proof surface and let it cool to room temperature. That's all there is to seasoning, and your pan is ready to go.

Please note that with use, your cast-iron grilling pan will darken. This is normal, and even beneficial, as the darkening indicates that the pores of the iron are sealing. The sealing creates a durable coating that prevents sticking.

Before you begin a recipe, set up the grilling pan. Adjust your broiler rack to position the food on the grilling pan about two to three inches from the heat source. Fill the drip pan (the bottom piece of the grilling pan) with $1/2$ inch of water, which will reduce smoke and prevent flareups. At least 10 minutes before you will begin cooking, set the pan in place and turn the broiler on to preheat. While you are cooking, it may be necessary to replenish the water in the drip pan, so keep an eye on it.

After cooking and cooling, your broiler grilling pan should never go in the dishwasher. Simply wash it with hot, soapy water using a nonabrasive cleaner and a plastic or nylon cleaning pad. Dry your pan with paper towels and then coat the entire cooking surface with a thin layer of solid vegetable shortening. Wipe the pan with a paper towel and you are ready to grill again.

As with stovetop grilling pieces, never run water on a broiling pan that is hot, which can cause warping. Also, never set a hot pan on a cold surface, which can also cause warping and possibly damage the surface.

COOKING TIPS

1. Thin and relatively tender foods are best suited to indoor grilling. Foods that are no more than 2 inches thick work best. To cook anything thicker than 2 inches you will need to

split it in half crosswise or ask your butcher to butterfly it.

2. When using bamboo skewers, immerse them in water for at least 30 minutes before threading food on them. Soaking will help to prevent the bamboo from burning.

3. Preheat the pan or griddle thoroughly and according to the manufacturer's instructions before cooking.

4. Spraying the grilling pan or griddle with vegetable oil cooking spray or brushing it lightly with vegetable oil will help you achieve more pronounced browning and searing.

5. Use a paper towel to pat excess moisture off foods before grilling; this will also promote maximum browning and searing.

6. Before grilling, brush off marinade particles such as chopped onion or garlic from the meat or fish—they will burn if left on. Near the end of cooking you may brush or sprinkle the marinade particles on the food, allowing just enough time for light charring.

7. When grilling indoors, baste with glazes or marinades only in the last 4 to 5 minutes of cooking, particularly if the glaze or marinade contains a sweetener such as honey or marmalade. If brushed on at the beginning of cooking, it may cause undesirable burning.

8. Burned-on food residue can ruin the taste of the best ingredients, so be sure to clean your grilling pan or griddle thoroughly after each use (follow instructions specific to the equipment).

Sticking to these simple guidelines will bring you success with indoor grilling recipes, and ensure that your stovetop or oven grilling pan will become a long-lasting feature of your kitchen.

Grilled Chicken Caesar Salad

3 garlic cloves

3 tablespoons olive oil

1 teaspoon grated lemon zest

½ teaspoon salt

½ teaspoon black pepper

12 slices French bread

¾ pound skinless, boneless
    chicken breast halves

3 tablespoons fresh lemon juice

6 to 8 anchovy fillets

2 tablespoons mayonnaise

8 cups Romaine lettuce,
    torn into bite-size pieces

¼ cup grated Parmesan cheese

Prepare the grill according to the manufacturer's instructions. Spray the grill with nonstick cooking spray.

Mince 1 of the garlic cloves. In a small bowl, mix together the minced garlic, 1 tablespoon of the oil, lemon zest, ¼ teaspoon of the salt, and ¼ teaspoon of the pepper. Lightly brush 1 side of each bread slice with a little of the oil mixture. Put the chicken on a plate and rub the remaining oil mixture over both sides. Set aside.

In a food processor, combine the lemon juice, anchovies, mayonnaise, and the remaining oil, salt, and pepper. With the machine running, drop the remaining garlic cloves through the feed tube and process until puréed. Scrape the dressing into a large salad bowl.

Grill the chicken for 8 to 10 minutes, turning once, or until cooked through. Transfer to a clean plate. On the stovetop grill, grill the bread for 1 to 2 minutes on each side, or until toasted. On the broiler grill, grill the bread for 1 to 2 minutes, without turning, or until toasted. Cut the slices in half crosswise.

Mix the chicken juices that have collected on the plate into the dressing. Cut the chicken on an angle into thin strips. Add the Romaine and Parmesan to the dressing and toss to coat. Add the toast and chicken, toss again, and serve. *Serves 4.*

Asian Chicken and Broccoli Salad

The large broiler grill or a stovetop grill works best with this recipe.

8 ounces linguine

⅓ cup orange juice

**¼ cup reduced-sodium
soy sauce**

¼ cup chili sauce

**2 teaspoons Oriental (dark)
sesame oil**

2 garlic cloves, minced

½ teaspoon ground ginger

4 scallions, thinly sliced

2 carrots, shredded

3 cups small broccoli florets

**1 pound skinless, boneless
chicken breast halves**

In a large pot of boiling water, cook the linguine according to the package directions until al dente. Drain and transfer to a large bowl. In a small bowl, combine the orange juice, soy sauce, chili sauce, oil, garlic, and ginger. Measure out ¼ cup of the orange juice mixture and set aside. Add the remaining orange juice mixture, the scallions, and carrots to the linguine and toss to coat. Set aside.

Prepare the grill according to the manufacturer's instructions. Spray the grill with nonstick cooking spray.

In a large bowl, toss the broccoli with 2 tablespoons of the reserved orange juice mixture. Thread the broccoli onto 8 skewers. Brush the remaining 2 tablespoons orange juice mixture over the chicken.

Grill the chicken for 8 to 10 minutes, turning once, or until cooked through. Remove the chicken from the grill. Add the broccoli to the grill. Grill the broccoli for 5 minutes on the broiler grill, for 8 minutes on the stovetop grill, turning once, or until crisp-tender.

Cut the chicken on an angle into thin strips and transfer to the bowl with the linguine. Push the broccoli off the skewers into the bowl and toss well to combine. Serve warm, at room temperature, or chilled. *Serves 4.*

Citrus-Marinated Chicken

Grate the zest from the lemons and orange. Squeeze the juice from the lemons and orange; set the juices aside. In a small bowl, combine the grated lemon and orange zests and the maple syrup. Set aside.

In a shallow bowl, thoroughly blend the reserved citrus juices, the oil, thyme, and pepper. Add the chicken and turn to coat completely. Cover the bowl with plastic wrap. Marinate in the refrigerator for at least 4 hours or overnight, turning the chicken occasionally.

Prepare the grill according to the manufacturer's instructions. Spray the grill with nonstick cooking spray.

Brush any particles off the chicken. Grill the chicken for 20 to 25 minutes, turning often, or until almost cooked through. Brush the chicken with some of the maple syrup mixture, turn, and grill for 1 minute. Brush the chicken with the remaining mixture, turn, and grill for 1 more minute. Transfer the chicken to a platter and serve. *Serves 4.*

2 lemons

1 orange

¼ cup maple syrup

1 tablespoon olive oil

2 teaspoons thyme

½ teaspoon black pepper

2½ pounds chicken wings and
drumsticks

Chicken Quesadillas

The large broiler grill or a stovetop grill works best with this recipe.

¾ **pound skinless, boneless chicken breast halves**

3 tablespoons fresh lime juice

Eight 8-inch flour tortillas

¾ **cup (3 ounces) shredded Monterey jack cheese**

½ **cup chopped fresh cilantro (optional)**

4 scallions, thinly sliced

½ **cup mild or medium-hot reduced-sodium prepared salsa**

In a small bowl, toss the chicken with the lime juice. Prepare the grill according to the manufacturer's instructions. Spray the grill with nonstick cooking spray. Grill the chicken for 8 to 10 minutes, turning once, or until cooked through. Remove the chicken and cut into thin slices.

Tear off four 24-inch lengths of heavy-duty foil, fold each in half to form a 12 x 18-inch rectangle, and spray each with nonstick cooking spray. Place 1 tortilla in the center of each rectangle. Dividing evenly, top each tortilla with the chicken, cheese, cilantro, if using, scallions, and salsa. Top with the remaining tortillas and seal the packets.

Grill the packets for 5 minutes, turning once, or until piping hot. Carefully open each packet, cut the quesadillas into quarters, and serve. *Serves 4.*

For a spicier quesadilla use pepper jack—Monterey jack cheese studded with jalapeños. You can also substitute white or yellow Cheddar for the jack cheese, if necessary.

Chicken with Red Chili Sauce

3 tablespoons reduced-sodium
soy sauce

6 scallions, thinly sliced

4 garlic cloves, crushed

1 tablespoon chopped fresh
ginger

1 ½ teaspoons chili powder

1 teaspoon ground coriander

½ teaspoon black pepper

4 skinless, boneless chicken
breast halves (about
1 pound total)

3 large red bell peppers, halved
lengthwise and seeded

¼ cup cider vinegar or
rice vinegar

½ teaspoon red pepper flakes

½ teaspoon salt

2 tablespoons plus 1 teaspoon
sugar

In a food processor, combine the soy sauce, scallions, 3 cloves of the garlic, ginger, chili powder, coriander, and black pepper and process until smooth. Transfer the mixture to a sturdy plastic bag. Add the chicken, squeeze the air out of the bag, seal, and marinate in the refrigerator for 30 minutes or for up to 12 hours.

Prepare the grill according to the manufacturer's instructions. Spray the grill with nonstick cooking spray. On the broiler grill, grill the bell peppers, cut sides down, for 10 minutes, or until charred. On the stovetop grill, grill the bell peppers for 15 to 18 minutes, turning once, or until charred. Remove the peppers and set them aside to cool slightly. Grill the chicken for 8 to 10 minutes, turning once, or until cooked through. Remove the chicken and keep it warm.

Meanwhile, when cool enough to handle, peel the bell pepper halves. Cut 2 of the pepper halves into thin strips and set aside. Add the remaining peppers to a food processor and purée. Combine the pepper purée, vinegar, red pepper flakes, the remaining clove of garlic, and the salt in a small saucepan. Bring to a boil over medium heat, stir in the sugar, and cook until the sugar has dissolved and the sauce is slightly syrupy, about 4 minutes. Stir the reserved pepper strips into the sauce.

Serve the chicken with the sauce on top. *Serves 4.*

Basil-Marinated Chicken

In a small saucepan, combine the vinegar, wine, shallots, mace, pepper, and basil. Bring to a simmer over medium heat and cook for 2 minutes. Sprinkle the chicken legs with the salt and place them in a shallow baking dish. Pour the marinade over the chicken and cover the dish with plastic wrap. Marinate in the refrigerator for 8 hours or overnight.

Prepare the grill according to the manufacturer's instructions. Spray the grill with nonstick cooking spray.

Brush any particles off the chicken. Grill the chicken for 20 to 24 minutes, turning once, or until cooked through. Transfer the chicken to a platter and serve. *Serves 4.*

The heady spice called mace comes from the same plant as nutmeg. Mace is the delicate, lacy fiber that coats the nutmeg kernel. The thin layer of mace is peeled off and either ground or sold in small pieces called blades. Because the two spices are so closely related, nutmeg makes a satisfactory substitute for mace. Allspice is another possible replacement.

¾ cup malt vinegar

½ cup dry white wine

2 large shallots, thinly sliced

2 teaspoons mace

⅛ teaspoon black pepper

2 tablespoons chopped fresh basil, or 2 teaspoons dried

4 whole chicken legs, skinned

¼ teaspoon salt

Lemon Chicken Kebabs

The large broiler grill or a stovetop grill works best with this recipe.

4 skinless, boneless chicken
    breast halves, each cut
    lengthwise into 4 strips
1 zucchini, cut into
    ½-inch-thick rounds
1 red bell pepper, cut into
    1-inch squares
1 teaspoon grated lemon zest
¼ cup fresh lemon juice
1 ½ teaspoons sugar
¾ teaspoon oregano
½ teaspoon salt
4 pita breads, each cut into
    quarters
1 ⅓ cups reduced-sodium
    chicken broth
2 garlic cloves, minced
½ teaspoon ground ginger
2 teaspoons cornstarch
2 tablespoons chopped parsley

Prepare the grill according to the manufacturer's instructions. Spray the grill with nonstick cooking spray.

In a large bowl, combine the chicken, zucchini, bell pepper, lemon zest, 2 tablespoons of the lemon juice, sugar, oregano, and ¼ teaspoon of the salt. Toss to coat completely.

Alternating ingredients, thread the zucchini, chicken, and bell pepper onto 8 skewers. Grill the kebabs for about 8 minutes, turning once, or until the chicken is cooked through.

Meanwhile, dividing evenly, wrap the pitas in 2 foil packets and place on the grill with the chicken. Heat for 5 minutes, turning once, or until warmed through.

In a medium saucepan, combine the broth, the remaining 2 tablespoons lemon juice, the garlic, ginger, and the remaining ¼ teaspoon salt. Bring to a boil over high heat and cook, uncovered, for 3 minutes. Combine the cornstarch and 1 teaspoon water, stir to blend, and stir into the boiling broth. Cook, stirring constantly, until the sauce is lightly thickened, about 1 minute. Stir in the parsley.

Serve the kebabs and pitas with the lemon sauce. *Serves 4.*

Barbecued Chicken with Tropical Fruit Salsa

20-ounce can juice-packed
    crushed pineapple

1 mango, peeled and diced

1/4 cup chopped fresh cilantro
    or parsley

1/4 cup chopped mango chutney

2 tablespoons fresh lemon juice

1/2 teaspoon salt

1/4 cup ketchup

2 teaspoons olive oil

1/2 teaspoon oregano

1/4 teaspoon allspice

1/8 teaspoon ground cloves

1/8 teaspoon cayenne pepper

4 skinless, boneless chicken
    breast halves

Drain the pineapple, reserving 1/4 cup of the juice. Transfer the pineapple to a large bowl and stir in the mango, cilantro, chutney, lemon juice, and 1/4 teaspoon of the salt.

In a small bowl, combine the reserved pineapple juice, the ketchup, oil, oregano, allspice, cloves, cayenne, and the remaining 1/4 teaspoon salt. Stir 1 tablespoon of the spiced ketchup into the pineapple-mango mixture, cover, and refrigerate until serving time.

Transfer the remaining spiced ketchup to a sturdy plastic bag. Add the chicken, squeeze the air out of the bag, seal, and marinate in the refrigerator for 30 minutes or for up to 2 hours.

Prepare the grill according to the manufacturer's instructions. Spray the grill with nonstick cooking spray.

Grill the chicken for 8 to 10 minutes, turning once, or until cooked through. Cut the chicken on an angle into thin strips. Serve the tropical fruit salsa alongside the chicken. *Serves 4.*

Your best guide to choosing a mango is its fragrance. A sweet, slightly flowery aroma should be detectable at the stem end. If the fruit does not yield to gentle finger pressure, keep it at room temperature for a few days until it becomes softer and more fragrant.

Lemon-Honey Chicken Breasts

In a shallow bowl, combine the lemon juice, honey, oil, soy sauce, and ginger. Add the chicken breasts, turn to coat, and let stand for 10 minutes.

Prepare the grill according to the manufacturer's instructions. Spray the grill with nonstick cooking spray.

Remove the chicken from the marinade, reserving the marinade.

Grill the chicken for 8 to 10 minutes, turning once and brushing with the reserved marinade, or until cooked through. Transfer the chicken to a platter and serve warm or at room temperature. *Serves 4.*

These chicken breasts are good fare for a picnic. Or use them sliced for sandwiches or cut into strips to add to a Caesar-type salad.

3 tablespoons fresh lemon juice

1 tablespoon honey

1 tablespoon vegetable oil

1 teaspoon soy sauce

¼ teaspoon ground ginger

4 skinless, boneless chicken breast halves

Onion-Smothered Chicken

6 tablespoons red wine vinegar

4 teaspoons sugar

$1/2$ teaspoon sage

$1/2$ teaspoon salt

4 skinless, boneless chicken
    breast halves

2 teaspoons olive oil

2 large onions, halved and
    thinly sliced

1 cup reduced-sodium
    chicken broth

1 tablespoon all-purpose flour

1 carrot, cut into thin strips

1 red bell pepper, cut into
    thin strips

$1/4$ teaspoon black pepper

In a shallow bowl, combine 3 tablespoons of the vinegar, 2 teaspoons of the sugar, $1/4$ teaspoon of the sage, and $1/4$ teaspoon of the salt and stir to blend. Add the chicken, turn to coat, cover, and refrigerate.

In a large skillet, warm the oil over medium heat. Add the onions and the remaining 2 teaspoons sugar and cook, stirring occasionally, until the onions begin to brown, about 5 minutes. Add the broth and cook until most of the liquid has evaporated, about 5 minutes. Stir in the flour, carrot, bell pepper, the remaining 3 tablespoons vinegar, the remaining $1/4$ teaspoon sage, the remaining $1/4$ teaspoon salt, and the black pepper and cook until the onions are tender and caramelized, about 10 minutes.

Meanwhile, prepare the grill according to the manufacturer's instructions. Spray the grill with nonstick cooking spray. Grill the chicken for 8 to 10 minutes, turning once, or until cooked through.

Place the chicken on 4 plates, spoon the onion mixture around the chicken, and serve. *Serves 4.*

Marinated, grilled chicken is punctuated by a relish of slowly-cooked sweet onion and tart red wine vinegar. Carrots and red pepper add accents of color and crunch.

Chicken Teriyaki

1 ½ tablespoons soy sauce

1 tablespoon honey

1 teaspoon ground ginger

½ teaspoon Oriental (dark)
  sesame oil

1 garlic clove, crushed

1 pound skinless, boneless
  chicken breasts, cut into
  2-inch pieces

⅔ cup rice

¼ teaspoon salt

1 green bell pepper, cut into
  1-inch squares

1 pint cherry tomatoes

2 scallions, finely chopped

In a shallow bowl, combine the soy sauce, honey, ginger, oil, and garlic and stir to blend. Add the chicken, toss to coat completely, and let stand while you start cooking the rice.

In a medium saucepan, combine the rice, 1 ⅓ cups water, and the salt. Bring to a boil over high heat, reduce the heat, and simmer, covered, until the rice is tender and all the water is absorbed, about 17 minutes.

Meanwhile, prepare the grill according to the manufacturer's instructions. Spray the grill with nonstick cooking spray. Alternating ingredients, thread pieces of chicken, bell pepper, and the tomatoes onto 8 skewers (if using a small broiler grill, use skewers no more than 8 inches long). Grill the kebabs for about 8 minutes, turning once, or until the chicken is cooked through.

Stir the scallions into the rice. Spoon the rice onto 4 plates, place the kebabs on top, and serve. *Serves 4.*

Chicken Dijon

Prepare the grill according to the manufacturer's instructions. Spray the grill with nonstick cooking spray.

In a 1-cup measure, combine the mustard, honey, and vinegar and stir to blend. Transfer 1/4 cup of the honey-mustard mixture to a medium bowl. Set the rest aside.

Add the zucchini, bell pepper, tomato, scallions, and black pepper to the 1/4 cup honey-mustard mixture and toss to coat completely.

Brush the chicken with the reserved honey-mustard mixture and grill for 8 to 10 minutes, turning once, or until cooked through.

Place the chicken on 4 plates, spoon the zucchini–bell pepper relish on top, and serve. *Serves 4.*

3 tablespoons Dijon mustard

2 tablespoons honey

4 teaspoons cider vinegar

1 small zucchini, sliced into 1-inch half-moons

1/2 small red bell pepper, cut into 1-inch squares

1 small tomato, finely diced

4 tablespoons finely chopped scallions

1/8 teaspoon black pepper

4 skinless, boneless chicken breast halves

Chicken with Spicy Peanut Sauce

6 quarter-size slices fresh ginger, unpeeled

2 garlic cloves, peeled

4 medium scallions, cut into 2 inch lengths

5 tablespoons soy sauce

1 tablespoon Oriental (dark) sesame oil

4 skinless, boneless chicken breast halves

⅓ cup creamy peanut butter

¼ cup chicken broth

¼ teaspoon red pepper flakes

1 teaspoon sugar

In a food processor, mince the ginger. Add the garlic and mince. Add the scallions and pulse on and off to finely chop.

In a large shallow dish, combine the scallion mixture with 3 tablespoons of the soy sauce and the oil. Add the chicken breasts and turn to coat completely. Cover the dish with plastic wrap and marinate in the refrigerator for 20 minutes.

Meanwhile, prepare the grill according to the manufacturer's instructions. Spray the grill with nonstick cooking spray.

In a small bowl, combine the peanut butter, broth, the remaining 2 tablespoons soy sauce, the red pepper flakes, and sugar. Set aside.

Grill the chicken for 8 to 10 minutes, turning once, or until cooked through.

Serve the chicken with the peanut sauce on top or on the side. *Serves 4.*

Grilled Turkey and Orange Salad

The large broiler grill or a stovetop grill works best with this recipe.

1 pound small red potatoes

½ pound green beans, trimmed

¼ cup orange juice

2 tablespoons orange marmalade

2 tablespoons maple syrup

½ teaspoon salt

½ teaspoon ground ginger

½ teaspoon grated orange zest

¼ teaspoon black pepper

1 pound boneless turkey breast,
   in one piece, butterflied

2 teaspoons Dijon mustard

1 tablespoon red wine vinegar

2 navel oranges, peeled and
   sectioned

4 cups red leaf lettuce

Prepare the grill according to the manufacturer's instructions. Spray the grill with nonstick cooking spray.

In a large pot of boiling water, cook the potatoes, about 10 minutes. Drain and cut the potatoes in half. Tear off a 24-inch length of heavy-duty foil and fold it in half to form a 12 x 18-inch rectangle. Place the beans and 2 tablespoons water on the foil and seal the packet. Set it aside.

In a large bowl, combine the orange juice, marmalade, maple syrup, salt, ginger, orange zest, and pepper. Measure out ¼ cup of the mixture to use as a baste; set the remainder aside.

On the broiler grill, grill the turkey for 20 minutes. Brush with the baste, turn, and grill for 2 to 3 minutes. Brush again, turn, and grill for 2 to 3 more minutes. On the stovetop grill, grill the turkey for 25 minutes. Brush with the baste, turn, and grill for 2 minutes. Brush again, turn, and grill for 2 more minutes. Remove the turkey from the grill and set aside.

Place the packet of beans and the potatoes on the grill for 10 minutes, turning once, or until the potatoes are cooked through.

Meanwhile, whisk the mustard and vinegar into the orange juice mixture left in the bowl. Add the orange sections and toss. Thinly slice the turkey. Add the turkey to the bowl along with the green beans, potatoes, and lettuce and toss. *Serves 4.*

Turkey Burgers

Prepare the grill according to the manufacturer's instructions. Spray the grill with nonstick cooking spray.

In a medium bowl, mix together the turkey, mustard, Worcestershire sauce, garlic, onion, salt, and pepper just until combined. Form into 4 patties.

Grill the patties for 8 to 9 minutes, turning once, or until they are firm and cooked through. Lay a piece of cheese on each burger. If using the stovetop grill, cover the burgers loosely with heavy-duty foil. Grill for about 30 seconds, or until the cheese is melted.

Place each burger on a roll and serve with lettuce, tomato, and onion, if using. *Serves 4.*

1 ¼ **pounds ground turkey**

1 **tablespoon Dijon mustard**

1 **tablespoon Worcestershire sauce**

2 **garlic cloves, minced**

1 **small onion, minced**

½ **teaspoon salt**

¼ **teaspoon black pepper**

4 **slices Monterey jack cheese**

4 **rolls, split and toasted**

Garnishes (optional):

Lettuce leaves

Tomato slices

Onion slices

Lime-Grilled Turkey Sandwiches

4 turkey cutlets (about
   ½ pound total), pounded
   ¼ inch thick, if necessary
¼ cup fresh lime juice
1 tablespoon olive oil
½ teaspoon salt
¼ teaspoon black pepper
⅓ cup mayonnaise
2 tablespoons chopped cilantro
   (optional)
1 teaspoon grated lime zest
   (optional)
1 small avocado
4 club rolls or other hard rolls
4 lettuce leaves
¼ cup cranberry sauce

Prepare the grill according to the manufacturer's instructions. Spray the grill with nonstick cooking spray.

Place the turkey cutlets in a shallow dish and sprinkle them with 2 tablespoons of the lime juice, the oil, salt, and pepper. Turn the cutlets to coat completely.

Grill the cutlets for 6 minutes, turning once, or until cooked through.

Meanwhile, in a small bowl, stir together 1 more tablespoon of the lime juice, the mayonnaise, and the cilantro and lime zest, if using.

Peel and slice the avocado and toss it with the remaining 1 tablespoon lime juice.

Split the rolls lengthwise and place them, cut sides toward the heat, on the grill for about 30 seconds, or until lightly toasted.

Spread both halves of each roll with the lime mayonnaise. Place a lettuce leaf and a turkey cutlet on half of each roll and top with the avocado slices and a spoonful of the cranberry sauce. *Serves 4.*

Grilled Turkey with Herb-Dijon Marinade

The large broiler grill or a stovetop grill works best with this recipe.

In a medium bowl, combine the scallions, yogurt, lemon juice, garlic, parsley, mustard, lemon zest, cumin, coriander, salt, black pepper, and cayenne.

Slice the turkey across the grain into 1/4-inch-thick slices.

Add the turkey to the bowl and toss to coat completely. Cover the bowl with plastic wrap and marinate in the refrigerator for at least 3 hours or overnight, tossing the turkey in the marinade occasionally.

Prepare the grill according to the manufacturer's instructions. Spray the grill with nonstick cooking spray.

Arrange the turkey slices in 1 layer on the grill. Grill the turkey for 8 to 10 minutes, turning once, or until golden and cooked through.

Transfer the turkey to a platter and serve. *Serves 8.*

Turkey is so lean that it can easily dry out when grilled. If you grill the turkey taken straight from the refrigerator (rather than letting it come to room temperature) it will be less likely to overcook. Spoon any marinade left in the bowl over the turkey when you first place it on the grill to help keep the meat moist.

3 scallions, coarsely chopped

1 cup plain low-fat yogurt

1/4 cup fresh lemon juice

4 garlic cloves, minced

1/4 cup chopped parsley

1 tablespoon Dijon mustard

2 teaspoons grated lemon zest

2 teaspoons cumin

2 teaspoons ground coriander

1/2 teaspoon salt

1/4 teaspoon black pepper

1/4 teaspoon cayenne pepper

1 skinless, boneless turkey breast half (about 2 3/4 pounds)

Grilled Sesame Shrimp on Skewers

I pound large shrimp

I ½ tablespoons soy sauce

I tablespoon fresh lemon juice

I tablespoon Oriental (dark)
    sesame oil

½ teaspoon minced fresh ginger

½ teaspoon cumin

2 teaspoons sesame seeds

Prepare the grill according to the manufacturer's instructions. Spray the grill with nonstick cooking spray.

Thread the shrimp onto 4 to 8 skewers, pushing the skewer through both the head and the tail of each shrimp (if using the small broiler grill, use skewers no more than 8 inches long).

In a small bowl, combine the soy sauce, lemon juice, oil, ginger, and cumin. Brush the mixture over both sides of the shrimp; then sprinkle with sesame seeds.

Grill the shrimp for 3 to 4 minutes, turning once, or until just opaque. Push the shrimp off the skewers, divide among 4 plates, and serve immediately. *Serves 4.*

You may grill the shrimp in the shell or out of the shell. To remove the shell, gently peel it off, starting underneath the shrimp. Use a paring knife to cut along the curved back of the shrimp where you see a dark line. Lift out this vein with the point of the knife and rinse the shrimp well.

Jamaican Jerked Shrimp with Pineapple

5 scallions, thinly sliced

2 tablespoons minced fresh
    ginger

3 garlic cloves, minced

2 teaspoons olive oil

$1/2$ teaspoon allspice

$1/2$ teaspoon black pepper

$1/4$ teaspoon cinnamon

$1/8$ teaspoon cayenne pepper

$3/4$ teaspoon salt

1 tablespoon firmly packed
    dark brown sugar

24 large shrimp (about 1 pound),
    shelled and deveined

20-ounce can juice-packed
    pineapple wedges, drained

1 large red bell pepper, diced

2 tablespoons fresh lime juice

2 tablespoons chopped
    fresh mint

In a large bowl, combine 4 of the scallions, 1 tablespoon plus 2 teaspoons of the ginger, the garlic, oil, allspice, black pepper, cinnamon, cayenne, $1/2$ teaspoon of the salt, and 1 teaspoon of the brown sugar. Add the shrimp and toss well to coat completely. Marinate in the refrigerator for 20 minutes or for up to 12 hours.

Prepare the grill according to the manufacturer's instructions. Spray the grill with nonstick cooking spray.

Meanwhile, in a medium bowl, combine the pineapple, bell pepper, lime juice, the remaining scallion, the remaining 1 teaspoon ginger, the remaining $1/4$ teaspoon salt, and the remaining 2 teaspoons brown sugar. Stir in the mint and set aside.

Grill the shrimp for 3 to 4 minutes, turning once, or until just opaque. Divide the shrimp among 4 plates and serve with the pineapple mixture on the side. *Serves 4.*

The Caribbean spice blend called "jerk" adds an intriguing mixture of hot (cayenne) and sweet (cinnamon and allspice) flavors to barbecued chicken, meat, and seafood. Jerk works deliciously on this shrimp—and a minty pineapple relish is the perfect Caribbean way to cool the fire.

Garlic-Lemon Shrimp

Prepare the grill according to the manufacturer's instructions. Spray the grill with nonstick cooking spray.

In a small saucepan, warm 2 tablespoons of the butter over medium heat until it is melted. Add the dill, scallions, garlic, lemon zest, if using, salt, and pepper. Stir in the lemon juice.

If desired, shell and devein the shrimp. Thread the shrimp onto skewers, pushing the skewer through both the head and the tail of each shrimp (if you're using the small broiler grill, use skewers no more than 8 inches long). Place the skewers on the grill. Brush with some of the garlic-lemon mixture.

Grill the shrimp for 1 to 2 minutes, or until they begin to turn white. Turn the shrimp, brush them with more of the garlic-lemon mixture, and grill for 1 to 2 minutes, or until just opaque.

Thoroughly blend the remaining 1 tablespoon butter with the flour. Return the remaining garlic-lemon mixture to medium-high heat and bring to a boil. Add the butter-flour mixture bit by bit, stirring well after each addition, and cook until the sauce has thickened slightly, 2 to 3 minutes.

Serve the shrimp with the sauce on the side. *Serves 4.*

3 tablespoons unsalted butter

¼ cup (packed) fresh dill sprigs, finely chopped, or 2 teaspoons dried

3 scallions, finely chopped

2 garlic cloves, minced or crushed

1 tablespoon grated lemon zest (optional)

¼ teaspoon salt

¼ teaspoon black pepper

½ cup fresh lemon juice

1 pound medium shrimp

2 teaspoons all-purpose flour

Grilled Shrimp and Asparagus Salad

2 tablespoons fresh lemon juice

2 teaspoons Dijon mustard

1 ½ teaspoons olive oil

¼ teaspoon salt

¼ cup chopped parsley

1 teaspoon grated lemon zest

1 garlic clove, minced

1 pound large shrimp, shelled
and deveined

1 pound asparagus, tough ends
trimmed, cut diagonally
into 2-inch lengths

½ cup finely diced red bell
pepper

1 tablespoon finely chopped
pecans

In a medium bowl, combine the lemon juice, mustard, oil, and salt. Set the dressing aside. In another medium bowl, combine the parsley, lemon zest, and garlic. Add the shrimp and toss to coat. Marinate for 20 minutes in the refrigerator.

Prepare the grill according to the manufacturer's instructions. Spray the grill with nonstick cooking spray.

Tear off a 24-inch length of heavy-duty foil and fold in half to form a 12 x 18-inch rectangle. Place the asparagus and 2 tablespoons water in the center of the rectangle and seal the packet. Grill the packet for 12 minutes, or until the asparagus is crisp-tender. Add the asparagus to the dressing.

Grill the shrimp for 3 to 4 minutes, turning once, or until just opaque. Add the shrimp to the asparagus and toss to coat completely. Transfer the mixture to a platter, sprinkle with the bell pepper and pecans, and serve warm, at room temperature, or chilled. *Serves 4.*

This delicious main course offers great flexibility for entertaining. It can be served when the shrimp are still hot from the grill, slightly cooled, or even chilled—whatever suits your schedule. If you are serving the salad chilled, you can prepare it up to 8 hours in advance.

Bay-Scented Skewered Swordfish

A stovetop grill works best for this recipe.

1 small onion, cut into
    ¼-inch-thick slices and
    separated into rings
¼ cup fresh lemon juice
4 teaspoons olive oil
½ teaspoon salt
½ teaspoon black pepper
1 ½ pounds swordfish steaks,
    cut 1 inch thick, skinned
    and cut into 1-inch cubes
20 large bay leaves
2 cups boiling water

In a deep bowl, combine the onion, 2 tablespoons of the lemon juice, 2 teaspoons of the oil, the salt, and pepper. Add the swordfish cubes and toss to coat completely. Cover the bowl with plastic wrap and marinate in the refrigerator for 4 hours, turning the fish occasionally.

Meanwhile, in a heat-proof bowl, cover the bay leaves with the boiling water and let them soak for 1 hour.

Prepare the grill according to the manufacturer's instructions. Spray the grill with nonstick cooking spray.

Drain the bay leaves and remove the swordfish cubes from the marinade. Remove the onions from the fish. Alternating ingredients, thread the fish and bay leaves onto four 10-inch metal skewers, pressing the pieces firmly together. Combine the remaining 2 tablespoons lemon juice and the remaining 2 teaspoons oil and brush the lemon oil evenly over the fish.

Grill the fish for 6 to 8 minutes, turning the skewers every minute or so, or until the flesh is opaque when tested with the tip of a knife. Transfer the skewers to a heated platter and serve immediately. Discard the bay leaves. *Serves 4.*

Swordfish in Apple-Tarragon Sauce

Prepare the grill according to the manufacturer's instructions. Spray the grill with nonstick cooking spray.

In a medium saucepan, warm 1 tablespoon of the oil over medium heat. Add the shallot and cook until it is translucent, 1 to 2 minutes. Add the tarragon, clam juice, apple juice, cornstarch mixture, 1/8 teaspoon of the salt, and 1/8 teaspoon of the pepper. Whisking constantly, bring the mixture to a boil and let it thicken. Reduce the heat to low and simmer the sauce for 2 to 3 minutes; set the pan aside.

Season the fish steaks with the remaining 1/8 teaspoon salt and 1/8 teaspoon pepper. Brush the steaks with the remaining 1 tablespoon oil. Grill the steaks for 6 to 8 minutes, turning once, or until the flesh is opaque when tested with the tip of a knife.

While the steaks are grilling, reheat the sauce over low heat.

Transfer the steaks to a heated platter and pour the warm apple-tarragon sauce over them. Garnish the platter with the apple wedges and serve immediately. *Serves 4.*

2 tablespoons vegetable oil

2 tablespoons finely chopped shallot

2 tablespoons chopped fresh tarragon, or 2 teaspoons dried

1/2 cup clam juice

1/4 cup unsweetened apple juice

1 1/2 teaspoons cornstarch blended with 1 tablespoon cold water

1/4 teaspoon salt

1/4 teaspoon black pepper

1 1/2 pounds swordfish steak, shark steak, or tuna steak, cut 1/2 inch thick, cut into 4 equal pieces

1 red apple, quartered, cored, and cut into thin wedges

1 yellow apple, quartered, cored, and cut into thin wedges

Swordfish with Lemon, Tomato, and Basil Sauce

3 tablespoons Dijon mustard

2 tablespoons fresh lemon juice

2 tablespoons olive oil

2 tablespoons grated Parmesan cheese

1 teaspoon chopped fresh basil

1/4 teaspoon salt

1/4 teaspoon black pepper

4 swordfish steaks (about 2 pounds total), cut 1/2 inch thick

4 medium tomatoes, 1 coarsely chopped and 3 thinly sliced

3 tablespoons chopped parsley

Prepare the grill according to the manufacturer's instructions. Spray the grill with nonstick cooking spray.

In a small bowl, stir together the mustard, lemon juice, oil, Parmesan, basil, salt, and pepper.

Place the swordfish steaks on the grill and brush them lightly with some of the basil basting sauce. Grill the steaks for 4 minutes on the broiler grill, for 5 minutes on the stovetop grill, or until opaque on top.

Meanwhile, add the chopped tomato and the parsley to the remaining basting sauce.

Turn the swordfish steaks and spoon the basting sauce over them. Grill for 2 minutes, or until the flesh is opaque when tested with the tip of a knife.

Arrange the sliced tomatoes on a platter and top them with the swordfish steaks. Spoon any remaining sauce over the steaks and serve immediately. *Serves 4.*

Marinated Tuna Steaks

1 orange

1 lime

3 tablespoons olive oil

2 garlic cloves, minced

1 tablespoon plus 1 teaspoon
    chopped thyme

4 tuna steaks (about 6 ounces
    each), cut 3/4 inch thick

4 tablespoons unsalted butter,
    at room temperature

Salt

Black pepper

Grate the zest of the orange. Put $1/2$ teaspoon of the zest in a small bowl and put the remaining zest in an 8-inch square glass baking dish. Grate the zest of the lime. Put $1/2$ teaspoon of the zest in the small bowl and the remaining zest in the baking dish. Squeeze the juices from the orange and lime into the baking dish. Add the oil, half of the garlic, and 1 tablespoon of the thyme. Whisk the mixture until well blended. Add the tuna steaks to the baking dish and turn them twice. Cover with plastic wrap and refrigerate for 1 to 2 hours, turning the steaks twice.

Add the butter, the remaining garlic, and the remaining 1 teaspoon thyme to the bowl containing the zests. Blend well. Lay a 6-inch strip of wax paper on a flat surface and spoon the butter onto one end of the paper. Roll up the paper, creating a log shape. Twist the ends and refrigerate until needed.

Prepare the grill according to the manufacturer's instructions. Spray the grill with nonstick cooking spray.

Grill the steaks for 5 to 6 minutes, turning once, or until the tuna is firm and slightly pink in the center when tested with the tip of a knife. Remove them from the grill and sprinkle both sides of the steaks with salt and pepper to taste.

Cut the butter log into 4 pieces, top each tuna steak with a round of butter, and serve. *Serves 4.*

Asian Grilled Tuna Salad

Prepare the grill according to the manufacturer's instructions. Spray the grill with nonstick cooking spray.

In a food processor, finely chop the ginger and garlic. Add the soy sauce, lime juice, oil, honey, lime zest, black pepper, and red pepper flakes and process until blended. Set aside half the mixture to use as a salad dressing.

Brush the tuna steaks generously with some of the remaining ginger-garlic baste. Grill them for 3 minutes. Turn the steaks and brush with any remaining baste. Grill for 2 to 3 minutes, or until the tuna is firm and slightly pink in the center when tested with the tip of a knife.

Divide the cabbage, lettuce, carrots, and bean sprouts evenly among 4 plates. Cut the tuna into ¾-inch chunks and place them on the salads. Pour the reserved salad dressing over all and sprinkle with the sesame seeds. Serve immediately. *Serves 4.*

4 quarter-size slices fresh ginger, each cut ¼ inch thick, unpeeled

2 garlic cloves

¼ cup reduced-sodium soy sauce

3 tablespoons fresh lime juice

2 tablespoons vegetable oil

1 tablespoon honey

1 teaspoon grated lime zest

¼ teaspoon black pepper

¼ teaspoon red pepper flakes

1¼ pounds tuna steaks, cut ¾ inch thick

4 cups (about 6 ounces) shredded napa or Chinese cabbage

4 cups (about ½ head) shredded red leaf lettuce

2 large carrots, peeled and cut into matchsticks

2 cups (about ¼ pound) bean sprouts, rinsed and patted dry

2 tablespoons sesame seeds, toasted if desired

Salmon Steaks with Pesto and Peppers

The large broiler grill or a stovetop grill works best with this recipe.

1 cup reduced-sodium chicken
   broth

5 garlic cloves, peeled

2 teaspoons olive oil

2 cups packed fresh basil leaves

2 tablespoons grated Parmesan
   cheese

2 tablespoons fine unseasoned
   dry breadcrumbs

1 tablespoon fresh lemon juice,
   plus 1 lemon, cut into
   wedges

1/2 teaspoon salt

1/4 teaspoon black pepper

2 cups frozen corn kernels,
   thawed

4 scallions, sliced

4 bell peppers, mixed colors,
   halved lengthwise and
   seeded, stems left on

4 salmon steaks (about 1 pound
   total), cut 1/2 inch thick

In a medium saucepan, combine the broth, garlic, and oil. Bring to a boil over medium-high heat and cook until reduced to about 1/4 cup, 12 to 15 minutes. Let cool slightly and place in a blender or food processor along with the basil, Parmesan, breadcrumbs, lemon juice, salt, and black pepper and process until the pesto is smooth. In a medium bowl, place the corn, scallions, and half of the pesto and toss to combine.

Prepare the grill according to the manufacturer's instructions. Spray the grill with nonstick cooking spray. Grill the pepper halves, cut sides toward the heat, for 8 minutes. Remove them from the grill, and spoon the corn mixture into them, dividing evenly.

Brush the salmon steaks lightly with some of the remaining pesto. Grill the salmon, turning once and basting liberally with the remaining pesto, for 5 to 6 minutes on the broiler grill, for 6 to 8 minutes on the stovetop grill, or until the salmon is firm and flakes in the center when tested with the tip of a knife. Return the bell peppers to the grill to warm for 1 minute.

Remove the salmon skin before eating. Serve the salmon and peppers with lemon wedges, if you like. *Serves 4.*

Cod with Tomato and Bell Pepper Relish

4 medium plum tomatoes

1 small red bell pepper

3 scallions

¼ cup fresh basil leaves or
   1½ teaspoons dried

2 tablespoons olive oil

2 tablespoons red wine vinegar
   or cider vinegar

½ teaspoon black pepper

¼ teaspoon salt

4 cod or halibut steaks (about
   1 pound total), cut ¾ inch
   thick

Prepare the grill according to the manufacturer's instructions. If using the broiler grill, line it with heavy-duty foil. Spray the grill (or foil) with nonstick cooking spray.

Coarsely chop the tomatoes and place them in a bowl. In a food processor, coarsely chop the bell pepper, scallions, and basil. Transfer the vegetable mixture to the bowl with the tomatoes and stir in the oil, vinegar, pepper, and salt until well combined. Strain the excess liquid from the tomato and bell pepper relish into a small bowl. Set the relish aside.

Place the fish steaks on the grill and brush them with some of the relish liquid. Grill the steaks for 3 minutes, turn them, and brush with more of the liquid. Grill the steaks for about 3 minutes, or until they are lightly colored and flake when tested with the tip of a knife.

Transfer the fish steaks to a heated platter and top each with some of the tomato and bell pepper relish. *Serves 4.*

Scallop and Vegetable Brochettes

Prepare the grill according to the manufacturer's instructions. Spray the grill with nonstick cooking spray.

In a small skillet or saucepan, warm the butter over medium heat until it is melted. Add the garlic and cook until fragrant, about 30 seconds. Remove from the heat and stir in the lemon juice, red pepper flakes, parsley, and lemon zest, if using.

Alternating ingredients, thread the squash, bell pepper, scallops, and tomatoes onto skewers (if using the small broiler grill, use skewers no more than 8 inches long). Brush the fish and vegetables with half the garlic butter.

Grill the fish and vegetables for 3 minutes. Turn the skewers, brush with the remaining garlic butter, and grill for 3 to 5 minutes, or until the scallops are cooked through and the vegetables are tender. Serve immediately. *Serves 4.*

To make the garlic butter in a microwave, combine the first six ingredients in a small bowl. Cook in the microwave on high (100%) for 1 minute and stir to combine thoroughly.

3 tablespoons unsalted butter

2 garlic cloves, minced or crushed

1 teaspoon fresh lemon juice

¼ teaspoon red pepper flakes

3 tablespoons chopped parsley

2 teaspoons grated lemon zest (optional)

1 large yellow squash, halved lengthwise and cut crosswise into ½-inch half-moons

1 large green bell pepper, cut into 1-inch squares

1 pound sea scallops, cut in half if very large

16 cherry tomatoes

Herbed Flounder Rolls

¼ cup plain low-fat yogurt

1 tablespoon reduced-fat
    mayonnaise

1 red bell pepper, finely diced

3 tablespoons chopped parsley

1 teaspoon tarragon

¾ teaspoon grated lemon zest

4 flounder fillets (each about
    6 ounces), any visible bones
    removed

2 tablespoons fresh lemon juice

½ teaspoon salt

¼ teaspoon black pepper

3 tablespoons fine unseasoned
    dry breadcrumbs

In a small bowl, combine the yogurt, mayonnaise, bell pepper, 1 tablespoon of the parsley, ¼ teaspoon of the tarragon, and ¼ teaspoon of the lemon zest. Cover and refrigerate until serving time.

Prepare the grill according to the manufacturer's instructions. If using the broiler grill, line it with heavy-duty foil. Spray the grill (or foil) with nonstick cooking spray.

Lay the flounder fillets flat, skinned side up. Season with the lemon juice, salt, and black pepper. In a small bowl, combine the breadcrumbs, the remaining 2 tablespoons parsley, the remaining ¾ teaspoon tarragon, and the remaining ½ teaspoon lemon zest. Sprinkle the mixture over the flounder and, starting from a short side, neatly roll up each fillet.

Arrange the rolls, seam sides down, on the grill (if using the stovetop grill, cover the fish with heavy-duty foil). Grill the rolls for 8 to 10 minutes, or until the fish is just opaque in the center. Place the rolls on 4 plates, top with the bell pepper–tartar sauce, and serve. *Serves 4.*

For a more traditional flavor, add 2 teaspoons minced dill pickle to the tartar sauce.

Grilled Sole Fillets with Cucumber-Dill Sauce

1 tablespoon unsalted butter, melted

¼ cup (packed) fresh dill sprigs, or 1 ½ teaspoons dried

½ teaspoon salt

½ teaspoon black pepper

1 cup plain low-fat yogurt

3 tablespoons fresh lemon juice

2 teaspoons grated lemon zest

½ teaspoon dry mustard

2-inch piece cucumber, peeled, seeded, and finely chopped

¼ cup finely chopped red bell pepper

4 small sole or other firm-fleshed white fish fillets (about 1 ½ pounds total)

Prepare the grill according to the manufacturer's instructions. If using the broiler grill, line it with heavy-duty foil. Spray the grill (or foil) with nonstick cooking spray.

In a small bowl, combine the melted butter with 1 tablespoon of the fresh dill, ¼ teaspoon of the salt, and ¼ teaspoon of the black pepper. Set aside.

In a serving bowl, combine the yogurt, lemon juice, lemon zest, mustard, the remaining 3 tablespoons fresh dill, the remaining ¼ teaspoon salt, and the remaining ¼ teaspoon black pepper. Stir in the cucumber and bell pepper. Set aside.

Brush the dill butter over both sides of the fillets. Grill the fillets for 4 to 5 minutes, turning once and brushing with the dill butter again (do not turn the fillets if using the broiler grill), or until the fish flakes when tested with the tip of a knife.

Divide the fillets among 4 heated plates and top each fillet with a generous dollop of cucumber-dill sauce. *Serves 4.*

Greek Lamb Kebabs with Mint Sauce

In a small bowl, combine the yogurt, half the mint, ¼ teaspoon of the salt, and ¼ teaspoon of the pepper. Cover and refrigerate until serving time.

In a large pot of boiling water, cook the orzo with ¼ teaspoon of the remaining salt until tender. Drain; stir in the remaining mint, the oil, and lemon zest. Set aside.

Meanwhile, in a shallow bowl, combine the lemon juice, garlic, oregano, the remaining ¼ teaspoon salt, and the remaining ¼ teaspoon pepper. Add the lamb and onion and toss to coat completely.

Prepare the grill according to the manufacturer's instructions. Spray the grill with nonstick cooking spray.

Alternating ingredients, thread the lamb, onion, and cherry tomatoes onto 8 skewers (if using the small broiler grill, use skewers no more than 8 inches long). Grill the kebabs for 8 minutes on the broiler grill, 10 minutes on the stovetop grill, turning occasionally, or until the lamb is cooked through.

Divide the orzo among 4 plates, place 2 kebabs on each plate, and serve with the mint sauce. *Serves 4.*

Rosemary is also excellent with lamb. For a change, try substituting it for the oregano.

½ **cup plain low-fat yogurt**
⅓ **cup chopped fresh mint**
¾ **teaspoon salt**
½ **teaspoon black pepper**
1¼ **cups orzo**
1 **teaspoon olive oil**
½ **teaspoon grated lemon zest**
3 **tablespoons fresh lemon juice**
2 **garlic cloves, minced**
1 **teaspoon oregano**
¾ **pound well-trimmed boneless lamb loin chops, cut into 16 chunks**
1 **red onion, cut into 16 chunks**
16 **cherry tomatoes**

Grilled Steaks with Red Wine–Mushroom Sauce

2 garlic cloves, minced or
   crushed

I cup dry red wine

2 tablespoons soy sauce

I tablespoon red wine vinegar

I teaspoon thyme

¼ teaspoon black pepper

4 New York strip or strip loin
   steaks (about 1¾ pounds
   total), cut ¾ to I inch thick

2 tablespoons unsalted butter

4 scallions, coarsely chopped

¾ pound mushrooms, thinly
   sliced

2 tablespoons all-purpose flour

In a shallow nonmetallic dish large enough to hold the steaks in a single layer, combine half the garlic, the wine, soy sauce, vinegar, thyme, and pepper. Place the steaks in the marinade and turn to coat completely. Cover the dish with plastic wrap. Marinate in the refrigerator for 2 to 3 hours, turning the steaks occasionally.

Prepare the grill according to the manufacturer's instructions. Spray the grill with nonstick cooking spray.

In a medium skillet, melt the butter over medium heat. Add the remaining garlic, the scallions, and mushrooms and cook until the scallions are limp and the mushrooms start to give up their liquid, 2 to 3 minutes. Stir in the flour and cook, stirring, until the flour is absorbed, about 30 seconds.

Remove the steaks from the marinade, reserving the marinade. Stir the reserved marinade into the skillet and cook, stirring, until the mixture has come to a boil and thickened slightly, 1 to 2 minutes. Reduce the heat to low and simmer while the steaks are grilling.

Grill the steaks for 3 to 4 minutes on each side for rare, 4 to 5 minutes on each side for medium-rare, 5 to 7 minutes on each side for well done, or until desired doneness. Let the steaks rest for 5 minutes before serving with the red wine–mushroom sauce. *Serves 4.*

Barbecued Spareribs

This recipe is appropriate only for a stovetop grill.

3 pounds spareribs

2 garlic cloves, chopped

½ medium onion, coarsely
    chopped

1 ½ pounds plum tomatoes,
    coarsely chopped

4 tablespoons unsalted butter

¼ teaspoon cumin

¼ teaspoon chili powder

2 teaspoons chopped parsley

¼ teaspoon cayenne pepper

½ teaspoon black pepper

2 teaspoons red wine vinegar

1 tablespoon fresh lemon juice

Half a 6-ounce can tomato paste

3 tablespoons liquid brown sugar
    or dark cane syrup

3 tablespoons dry red wine

Prepare the grill according to the manufacturer's instructions, preheating it over low heat.

Arrange the ribs in a single layer on the grill. Grill the ribs for 20 minutes, turning often, or until the ribs lose their raw look.

Meanwhile, in a large saucepan, combine the garlic, onion, tomatoes, butter, cumin, chili powder, parsley, cayenne, black pepper, vinegar, and lemon juice. Bring to a simmer over low heat; cover and cook, stirring occasionally, for 15 minutes. Uncover the pan and add the tomato paste, liquid brown sugar and wine. Return to a simmer and cook, stirring, until the mixture is thick and smooth, about 5 minutes. Remove from the heat. Pour the sauce into a blender or food processor and blend until smooth, about 45 seconds. Transfer the sauce to a large mixing bowl.

Brush the ribs with the barbecue sauce and grill for about 25 minutes, turning occasionally, or until the ribs are crusty with sauce and have turned a dark brick-red color.

Transfer the ribs to a platter and serve. *Serves 4.*

Beef Tenderloin Steaks with Roasted Garlic Sauce

Preheat the oven to 500°F.

Scatter the garlic cloves in a small baking dish and roast them for 20 to 30 minutes, or until they are very soft. Set the garlic cloves aside to cool.

Prepare the grill according to the manufacturer's instructions. Spray the grill with nonstick cooking spray.

Press the pepper into both sides of the steaks and set them aside at room temperature.

Combine the wine and shallots in a small saucepan. Boil the mixture over medium-high heat until nearly all of the liquid has evaporated, about 5 minutes. Add the broth, bring the liquid to a boil, and continue cooking until it is reduced to about 1 cup, about 5 minutes.

Squeeze the garlic pulp from the skins into a food processor or a blender. Pour in the broth mixture and purée. Transfer the garlic sauce (it will be thick) to the saucepan and keep it warm.

Grill the steaks for 3 to 4 minutes on each side for medium-rare, or until desired doneness. Transfer the steaks to 4 plates and top with the garlic sauce. *Serves 4.*

2 whole garlic bulbs, cloves separated but not peeled

1 teaspoon black peppercorns, crushed

4 beef tenderloin steaks (about 1 ¼ pounds total), cut 1 inch thick

1 cup red wine vinegar

3 shallots, sliced or ½ small onion, finely chopped

2 cups reduced-sodium chicken broth

Dijon Burgers with Grilled Onions

1 pound lean ground beef

½ cup fine unseasoned dry breadcrumbs

¼ cup plus 2 tablespoons Dijon mustard

¼ cup dry red wine

1 large egg

2 teaspoons tarragon

½ teaspoon black pepper

2 tablespoons olive oil

1 large red onion, cut crosswise into ½-inch rounds

1 large yellow onion, cut crosswise into ½-inch rounds

Prepare the grill according to the manufacturer's instructions. Spray the grill with nonstick cooking spray.

In a medium bowl, combine the beef, breadcrumbs, 2 tablespoons of the mustard, 3 tablespoons of the red wine, the egg, 1 teaspoon of the tarragon, and ¼ teaspoon of the pepper. Mix briefly, just to distribute the breadcrumbs and seasonings (do not overmix). Shape the meat mixture into 4 patties.

In a small bowl, combine the remaining ¼ cup mustard, the remaining 1 tablespoon red wine, the remaining 1 teaspoon tarragon, the remaining ¼ teaspoon pepper, and the oil. Whisk to blend well.

Brush the burgers and onion slices with half the mustard mixture and grill for 4 minutes on the broiler grill, 5 minutes on the stovetop grill. Turn the burgers and onions and brush them with the remaining mustard mixture. Grill for 2 to 4 minutes for medium-rare, 4 to 5 minutes for medium, 6 to 7 minutes for well done, or until desired doneness.

Place each burger on a plate and top each with some of the onion slices. *Serves 4.*

Mexican Beef on Skewers

¼ **cup finely chopped onion**

I garlic clove, crushed

**I or 2 red chili peppers, seeded
and finely chopped**

½ **teaspoon cumin**

½ **tablespoon chopped fresh
oregano, or** ½ **teaspoon
dried**

½ **teaspoon paprika**

I tablespoon sesame seeds

**2 tablespoons finely chopped
cilantro**

I ½ **tablespoons vegetable oil**

I tablespoon fresh lime juice

2 bay leaves

I ¼ **pounds round steak, cut
into thin strips 6 inches long**

¼ **teaspoon salt**

I lime, cut into 8 wedges

In a shallow dish or pie plate, combine the onion, garlic, chili peppers, cumin, oregano, paprika, sesame seeds, cilantro, oil, lime juice, and bay leaves.

Place the beef strips in the marinade and stir to coat completely. Cover the dish with plastic wrap and marinate the meat in the refrigerator for 4 hours or overnight, turning the meat once or twice.

Prepare the grill according to the manufacturer's instructions. Spray the grill with nonstick cooking spray.

Thread the strips of meat onto 8 skewers (if using the small broiler grill, use skewers no more than 8 inches long). Sprinkle the meat with any remaining marinade. Grill the meat for 5 to 8 minutes, turning often, or until desired doneness.

Transfer the skewers to a serving platter and sprinkle with the salt. Serve the meat garnished with the lime wedges. *Serves 4.*

Grilled Pepper Steaks

The large broiler grill or a stovetop grill works best with this recipe.

Prepare the grill according to the manufacturer's instructions. Spray the grill with nonstick cooking spray.

Season the meat lightly with the salt; then pat the pepper firmly onto both sides of the steaks. Set aside.

Thread the mushroom caps onto 4 skewers by piercing through the center of each cap at an angle. Brush the mushrooms with the oil.

Arrange the mushroom skewers, cap sides down, on the grill. Grill the mushrooms, turning once, for about 3 minutes, or until tender and lightly browned. Remove from the grill.

Grill the steaks for 3 to 4 minutes on each side for medium-rare, or until desired doneness.

Serve each steak with a skewer of mushrooms. *Serves 4.*

4 beef tenderloin steaks (about 1 ¼ pounds), cut 1 inch thick
½ teaspoon salt
1 tablespoon coarsely ground black peppercorns
¾ pound fresh shiitake mushrooms, stemmed
2 teaspoons olive oil

Marinated London Broil

1 medium onion, coarsely
    chopped

1 tablespoon grated lemon zest

¼ cup fresh lemon juice

½ cup red wine vinegar

2 tablespoons olive oil

2 tablespoons Dijon mustard

3 garlic cloves, minced

1 ½ teaspoons basil

½ teaspoon black pepper

1 ½ pounds London broil, cut
    1 ¼ inches thick

In a shallow baking dish large enough to hold the steak, combine the onion, lemon zest, lemon juice, vinegar, oil, mustard, garlic, basil, and pepper.

Place the steak in the dish and spoon some of the marinade over the top. Cover the dish with plastic wrap and marinate the meat in the refrigerator for 8 hours or overnight, turning the steak every few hours.

Prepare the grill according to the manufacturer's instructions. Spray the grill with nonstick cooking spray.

Remove the steak from the marinade and brush off any particles. Grill the meat for 7 minutes. Turn the steak and, if using the stovetop grill, grill for 7 minutes for rare, 9 minutes for medium-rare, 11 minutes for medium to well done; if using the broiler grill, grill for 11 minutes for rare, 13 minutes for medium-rare, 15 minutes for medium to well done, or until desired doneness.

Let the steak stand for 5 minutes before carving it into thin slices. *Serves 6.*

*The lemon-mustard-garlic marinade could serve as background for
other herbs. Oregano would be a natural with the garlicky sauce;
tarragon or rosemary would also make a very tasty marinade.*

Ginger-Rubbed Steak

The large broiler grill or a stovetop grill works best with this recipe.

**2 teaspoons chopped fresh
 ginger**
⅛ teaspoon cayenne pepper
**2¾ pounds boneless sirloin
 steak, cut 1 inch thick**
¼ teaspoon salt

Prepare the grill according to the manufacturer's instructions. Spray the grill with nonstick cooking spray.

Rub the ginger and cayenne onto the steak, wrap it in plastic wrap and refrigerate for 30 minutes.

Grill the steak for 2 to 3 minutes on the stovetop grill, 4 minutes on the broiler grill. Turn the meat and sprinkle it with the salt. Grill the steak for 3 to 4 minutes on the stovetop grill, 4 to 5 minutes on the broiler grill, for medium-rare, or until desired doneness.

Transfer the steak to a platter and let it rest for 5 minutes before carving it into thin slices. *Serves 6.*

Grilled Spiced Pork Chops with Chutney

In a small bowl, combine 1/2 teaspoon of the salt, the sage, 1/2 teaspoon of the ginger, the allspice, garlic, and pepper. Rub the mixture onto the pork chops, wrap them in plastic wrap, and refrigerate for at least 10 minutes or for up to 12 hours.

Prepare the grill according to the manufacturer's instructions. Spray the grill with nonstick cooking spray. Grill the chops for 10 minutes on the broiler grill, 12 minutes on the stovetop grill, turning once, or until cooked through.

Meanwhile, in a medium saucepan, combine the apple juice, jam, vinegar, squash, curry powder, the remaining 1 teaspoon ginger, and the remaining 1/4 teaspoon salt. Cook over medium heat for 8 minutes. Add the apple, prunes, and scallions and cook until the apple and squash are tender, about 4 minutes.

Place the pork chops on 4 plates and serve with the chutney. *Serves 4.*

You can substitute the same amount of dark or golden raisins or finely chopped figs for the prunes.

- **3/4 teaspoon salt**
- **1/2 teaspoon sage**
- **1 1/2 teaspoons ground ginger**
- **1/4 teaspoon allspice**
- **2 garlic cloves, minced**
- **1/4 teaspoon black pepper**
- **4 well-trimmed pork loin chops (about 4 ounces each)**
- **3/4 cup apple juice**
- **2 tablespoons apricot or peach jam**
- **1 tablespoon cider vinegar**
- **1 1/2 cups diced butternut squash**
- **1 teaspoon curry powder**
- **1 Granny Smith apple, cored and cut into 1/2-inch chunks**
- **1/2 cup coarsely chopped prunes**
- **2 scallions, finely chopped**

Garlic and Rosemary Veal Chops

The large broiler grill or a stovetop grill works best with this recipe.

2 tablespoons olive oil

1 teaspoon grated lemon zest

2 tablespoons fresh lemon juice

2 large garlic cloves, finely
    chopped

3 shallots, finely chopped

1 tablespoon chopped parsley

1 teaspoon chopped fresh
    rosemary, or ½ teaspoon
    dried

Pinch of black pepper

4 veal rib chops (about 2 pounds
    total), cut ½ inch thick and
    cut between the bones

1 fennel bulb, cut into thin
    matchsticks

Lemon wedges

Prepare the grill according to the manufacturer's instructions. Spray the grill with nonstick cooking spray.

In a small bowl, combine the oil, lemon zest, lemon juice, garlic, shallots, parsley, rosemary, and pepper.

Brush the veal chops with about a quarter of the lemon-shallot mixture and grill for about 3 minutes, or until golden brown. Turn the chops and brush with another quarter of the lemon-shallot mixture. Grill for 3 minutes, or until desired doneness.

Meanwhile, in a small skillet, warm the remaining lemon-shallot mixture over medium heat. Add the fennel and cook, stirring, until golden brown, about 4 minutes.

Transfer the veal chops to a platter and top them with the fennel mixture. Garnish with the lemon wedges and serve. *Serves 4.*

Apricot-Glazed Beef Kebabs

½ cup apricot nectar

¼ cup dry white wine

2 tablespoons honey

1 teaspoon grated lime zest

2 tablespoons fresh lime juice

1 garlic clove, minced

1 teaspoon oregano

1 pound well-trimmed bottom
    round of beef, cut into
    1-inch cubes

16 dried apricot halves

¾ pound sweet potatoes, peeled
    and cut into 16 chunks

8 small white onions, halved

1 zucchini, cut into 16 pieces

In a sturdy plastic bag, combine the apricot nectar, wine, honey, lime zest, lime juice, garlic, and oregano. Add the beef and apricots, squeeze the air out of the bag, seal, and marinate in the refrigerator for 30 minutes or for up to 12 hours.

Meanwhile, in a large pot of boiling water, cook the sweet potatoes and onions until the potatoes are firm-tender, about 8 minutes. Drain.

Prepare the grill according to the manufacturer's instructions. Spray the grill with nonstick cooking spray.

Alternating ingredients, thread the beef, apricots, onions, sweet potatoes, and zucchini onto 8 skewers (if using the small broiler grill, use skewers no more than 8 inches long). Grill the kebabs for 12 to 15 minutes, turning occasionally, or until the beef is desired doneness.

Arrange the kebabs on a platter and serve. *Serves 4.*

You can substitute apple juice or chicken stock for the wine if you like.

Apricots, sweet potatoes, and onions make a sophisticated taste combination when added to beef kebabs. Although kebabs are often served for casual dining, this simple recipe is perfect for a dinner party. White or brown rice, tossed with diced carrots and minced fresh parsley or mint, makes a fine side dish.

Grilled Curried Beef

¾ cup plain low-fat yogurt

1½ teaspoons curry powder

¾ teaspoon ground ginger

½ teaspoon sugar

½ teaspoon salt

1 pound well-trimmed flank
    steak

1 cup long-grain rice

2 garlic cloves, minced

1 small yellow onion, cut into
    ½-inch-thick slices

1 ripe banana, cut into chunks

2 tablespoons tomato paste

2 teaspoons fresh lemon juice

In a small bowl, combine the yogurt, curry powder, ginger, sugar, and ¼ teaspoon of the salt. Measure out ¼ cup of the mixture and set aside. Rub the remaining yogurt mixture onto the flank steak. Wrap the steak in plastic wrap and marinate in the refrigerator for 30 minutes or for up to 12 hours.

Meanwhile, in a medium saucepan, bring 2¼ cups water and the remaining ¼ teaspoon salt to a boil. Add the rice and garlic. Reduce to a simmer, cover, and cook until the rice is tender, about 17 minutes.

Meanwhile, prepare the grill according to the manufacturer's instructions. Spray the grill with nonstick cooking spray. Grill the steak and onion for 10 minutes, turning once, or until the meat is desired doneness.

Let the steak stand for 5 minutes before slicing. Meanwhile, in a food processor, combine the onion, banana, tomato paste, lemon juice, and the reserved ¼ cup yogurt mixture and purée until smooth. Divide the rice among 4 plates, top with the steak and onion sauce, and serve. *Serves 4.*

Garlic-Mozzarella Bread

Prepare the grill according to the manufacturer's instructions.

In a small bowl, blend the butter, parsley, garlic, salt, and pepper.

Slice the bread lengthwise in half and spread the butter mixture over the cut sides, leaving a ¼-inch border all around. Sprinkle 1 piece of the bread with the mozzarella. Press the 2 pieces together and wrap them in heavy-duty foil.

On the stovetop grill, grill the bread for 3 to 4 minutes on each of 4 sides, or until the cheese has melted. On the broiler grill, grill the bread for 8 to 10 minutes, turning once, or until the cheese has melted.

Remove the bread from the foil, cut it into slices, and serve. *Serves 4.*

4 tablespoons unsalted butter, at
room temperature

3 tablespoons chopped parsley

2 garlic cloves, minced

¼ teaspoon salt

¼ teaspoon black pepper

1 loaf crusty Italian or French
bread (about 12 inches long)

½ cup (2 ounces) shredded
mozzarella cheese

Grilled Eggplant with Feta and Pasta

The large broiler grill or a stovetop grill works best with this recipe.

8 ounces small pasta shells

I pound plum tomatoes, coarsely
   chopped

⅓ cup chopped fresh mint

½ cup (2 ounces) crumbled
   feta cheese

2 teaspoons olive oil

I teaspoon salt

¼ cup balsamic vinegar

2 teaspoons firmly packed light
   brown sugar

I pound eggplant, peeled and
   cut lengthwise into
   ½-inch-thick slices

I zucchini, cut lengthwise into
   ½-inch-thick slices

I red bell pepper, halved
   lengthwise and seeded

Prepare the grill according to the manufacturer's instructions. Spray the grill with nonstick cooking spray.

In a large pot of boiling water, cook the pasta according to the package directions until al dente. Drain. In a large bowl, combine the tomatoes, mint, feta, oil, and salt. Add the pasta and toss to coat completely. Set the pasta aside.

In a small bowl, combine the vinegar and brown sugar. Brush the eggplant and zucchini with half the vinegar mixture.

Place the eggplant, zucchini, and bell pepper (arrange the pepper cut sides down) on the grill. On the broiler grill, grill for 10 minutes, turning only the eggplant and zucchini, or until the eggplant and zucchini are tender and the bell pepper is charred. On the stovetop grill, grill the eggplant and zucchini for 10 minutes and the bell pepper for 15 to 18 minutes, turning the vegetables once, or until the eggplant and zucchini are tender and the bell pepper is charred.

Cut the eggplant and zucchini into 1-inch pieces and toss with the pasta. Peel the bell pepper, cut it into large squares, and toss with the pasta along with the remaining vinegar mixture. Divide the mixture among 4 plates and serve at room temperature. *Serves 4.*

Roasted Red Pepper, Snow Pea, and Tomato Salad

3 small red bell peppers (about ¾ pound total), halved lengthwise and seeded

¼ pound snow peas, strings removed, or tiny green beans

1 tablespoon Dijon mustard

½ teaspoon Creole mustard

2 scallions, finely chopped

2 tablespoons tarragon vinegar or white wine vinegar

¼ cup minced fresh tarragon or oregano, loosely packed, or 1 teaspoon dried

½ cup olive oil

Salt

Black pepper

1 small head of Boston lettuce, separated into leaves

2 tomatoes (about 1 pound), cut into ½-inch-thick slices

Prepare the grill according to the manufacturer's instructions.

On the broiler grill, grill the bell peppers, cut sides down, for 10 minutes, or until charred. On the stovetop grill, grill the bell peppers for 15 to 18 minutes, turning once, or until charred. Set them aside to cool.

In a saucepan, cook the snow peas in boiling water until blanched, about 2 minutes. Drain them in a colander and rinse them under cold water; pat them dry with paper towels and set them aside.

In a bowl, combine the Dijon mustard, Creole mustard, scallions, vinegar, and tarragon and whisk until smooth. Gradually drizzle in the oil, whisking constantly, until the dressing is thick and smooth and the consistency of mayonnaise. Add salt and pepper to taste.

Peel the bell pepper halves and cut them into ½-inch-wide strips. Line a platter with the lettuce leaves and arrange the tomatoes, snow peas, and bell pepper strips decoratively on top. Pour the dressing over the salad. *Serves 4.*

Grilled Stuffed Mushrooms

In a large bowl, combine the broth, mustard, lemon juice, and Worcestershire sauce. Add the mushroom caps and toss to coat completely. Marinate at room temperature for 30 minutes.

Prepare the grill according to the manufacturer's instructions. Spray the grill with nonstick cooking spray.

Reserving the marinade, drain the mushroom caps and set them aside. Coarsely chop the mushroom stems and place them in a large bowl. Add the bread, parsley, scallions, garlic, salt, and oil. Add the reserved marinade to the bread mixture and stir to moisten thoroughly.

Grill the mushrooms, stemmed sides down, for 5 minutes, or until lightly browned. Transfer the mushrooms to a flat surface, turn them stemmed sides up, and spoon the stuffing mixture into them, patting it down lightly. Return the mushrooms to the grill. If using the stovetop grill, cover the mushrooms with heavy-duty foil and grill for 8 minutes, or until the stuffing is piping hot. If using the broiler grill, grill the mushrooms for 6 to 7 minutes, or until lightly browned.

Arrange the mushrooms on a platter and serve warm.

Serves 4.

1 cup reduced-sodium chicken broth

3 tablespoons Dijon mustard

2 tablespoons fresh lemon juice

½ teaspoon Worcestershire sauce

12 large mushrooms, stems removed and reserved

4 ounces Italian or French bread, crumbled

½ cup chopped parsley

4 scallions, thinly sliced

2 garlic cloves, minced

½ teaspoon salt

1 teaspoon olive oil

Grilled Tomato-Basil Toasts

½ **loaf crusty Italian bread or**
   French baguette (about 8
   inches long)
1 **tablespoon mayonnaise**
1 **tablespoon olive oil**
1 **tablespoon tomato paste**
2 **tablespoons chopped fresh**
   basil, or 2 teaspoons dried
1 **garlic clove, minced**
⅛ **teaspoon salt**
⅛ **teaspoon black pepper**

Prepare the grill according to the manufacturer's instructions.

Slice the bread about ½ inch thick; then cut the slices in half.

In a small bowl, blend the mayonnaise, oil, tomato paste, basil, garlic, salt, and pepper.

On the stovetop grill, grill the bread for 1 to 2 minutes on each side, or until lightly toasted. On the broiler grill, grill the bread for 1 to 2 minutes, without turning, or until lightly toasted. Spread the tomato-basil mixture over each piece of bread and serve warm. *Serves 4.*

Herbed Summer Squash with Onions

2 tablespoons olive oil

1 small onion, minced

1 tablespoon basil

1 tablespoon oregano

1/2 teaspoon salt

1/4 teaspoon black pepper

2 medium zucchini, diced
    1/4 inch thick

2 medium yellow summer
    squash, diced 1/4 inch thick

Prepare the grill according to the manufacturer's instructions. Cut four 12-inch squares of heavy-duty foil.

In a medium bowl, combine the oil, onion, basil, oregano, salt, and pepper. Add the zucchini and yellow squash and toss to coat completely.

Stack 2 of the foil squares and turn the sides up to form a box. Repeat with the remaining foil squares. Reserving the marinade in the bowl, divide the squash mixture between the 2 boxes, fold the edges of the packets together, and crimp to seal tight. Grill for 12 to 15 minutes, turning once, or until the squash is tender but not mushy.

Return the squash mixture to the bowl. Serve immediately. *Serves 4.*

Grilling squash in a foil packet seals in all the delicious juices. Even if you are cooking in the winter, basil and oregano add fresh flavors that taste of summer.

Grilled Asparagus Parmesan

The large broiler grill or a stovetop grill works best with this recipe.

2 pounds thick asparagus, tough
    ends trimmed
¼ cup chicken broth
½ teaspoon grated lemon zest
½ teaspoon thyme
½ teaspoon salt
3 tablespoons grated Parmesan
    cheese

Prepare the grill according to the manufacturer's instructions. Spray the grill with nonstick cooking spray.

Tear off two 30-inch lengths of heavy-duty foil and fold each in half to form two 15 x 18-inch rectangles. Place half the asparagus in the center of each piece of foil. Fold the edges of the foil up a bit to form a lip and pour in half the broth. Sprinkle each portion with half the lemon zest, thyme, and salt and seal the packets.

Grill the packets for 12 minutes, or until the asparagus is just crisp-tender. Carefully open the packets and, using tongs, transfer the asparagus to the grill. Grill for 3 minutes, or until lightly browned.

Transfer the asparagus to a platter, sprinkle with the Parmesan, and serve. *Serves 4.*

Thicker asparagus often benefit from having the tough skin on the lower part of the stalk peeled off. Use a swivel-bladed vegetable peeler to remove the peel from the bottom half of the stalks after trimming the tough, white ends.

Herbed New Potatoes, Carrots, and Scallions

Prepare the grill according to the manufacturer's instructions.

In a large bowl, combine the potatoes, carrots, and scallions. Drizzle them with the oil and toss to coat evenly. Sprinkle the vegetables with sage and toss again.

Cut four 12-inch squares of heavy-duty foil. With a spoon, transfer the vegetables, dividing evenly, to the lower half of each piece of foil, arranging them in a single layer. Fold down the top half of the square, being careful not to disturb the vegetables, and crimp the edges to seal.

Grill the packets for 30 minutes, turning once, or until the vegetables are tender.

To serve, open the packets and turn the vegetables into a heated serving bowl. Season with salt and pepper. *Serves 4.*

16 small new potatoes (about
2 pounds total)
12 baby finger carrots (about
1/2 pound total)
9 scallions, trimmed, leaving
2 inches of green
1/2 cup olive oil
1 tablespoon minced fresh sage,
rosemary, or thyme, or
1 teaspoon dried
Salt
Black pepper

Grilled Potato Medley

This recipe is appropriate only for a stovetop grill.

2 baking potatoes (about 8
    ounces each)
2 sweet potatoes (about 8
    ounces each)
2 garlic cloves, peeled and halved
¼ cup chicken broth
2 teaspoons olive oil
½ teaspoon rosemary
½ teaspoon salt

Prepare the grill according to the manufacturer's instructions.

In a large pot of boiling water, cook the baking potatoes and sweet potatoes until almost tender, about 15 minutes. When cool enough to handle, slice the potatoes lengthwise ½ inch thick. Rub the potatoes with the garlic cloves. In a shallow bowl, combine the broth, oil, and rosemary. Add the potatoes and toss to coat.

Grill the potatoes for 12 minutes, turning occasionally, or until crisp outside and tender inside. Sprinkle with the salt and serve. *Serves 4.*

Both sweet and white potatoes should be stored at cool, but not cold, temperatures. Do not keep them in the refrigerator, as sweet potatoes will turn bland and white potatoes will develop an unappealing sweetness.

Apples with Apricot-Nut Stuffing

4 large apples, cored and peeled

3 tablespoons fresh lemon juice

2 tablespoons apricot spreadable fruit

2 tablespoons chopped dried apricots

I tablespoon finely chopped walnuts

Cut each apple in half lengthwise and cut a thin slice from the back of each apple half. In a medium bowl, toss the apple halves with 2 tablespoons of the lemon juice.

Prepare the grill according to the manufacturer's instructions.

In a small bowl, combine the spreadable fruit, chopped apricots, walnuts, and the remaining 1 tablespoon lemon juice.

Tear off two 24-inch lengths of heavy-duty foil, fold each in half to form a 12 x 18-inch rectangle, and spray each with non-stick cooking spray. Place 4 apple halves in the center of each rectangle. Dividing evenly, spoon the apricot-nut stuffing into each apple half and seal the packets.

Grill the packets for 8 to 10 minutes, or until the apples are tender. Serve hot, warm, or at room temperature. *Serves 4.*

If you don't have any lemons on hand, you can substitute orange juice for the lemon juice.

Grilled Stuffed Peaches

In a large pot of boiling water, cook the peaches until blanched, about 30 seconds. Rinse them under cold water and carefully remove their skins. With a sharp knife, halve and pit the peaches and cut a very thin slice from the rounded side of each peach half. In a medium bowl, toss the peach halves with the lemon juice.

Prepare the grill according to the manufacturer's instructions. Spray the grill with nonstick cooking spray.

Meanwhile, in a small bowl, combine the oats, brown sugar, almonds, butter, and cinnamon. Dividing evenly, fill the centers of each peach half with the stuffing. If using the stovetop grill, cover the peaches with heavy-duty foil.

Grill the peach halves for 5 to 8 minutes, or until tender. Place the peach halves on 4 plates and serve hot or warm. *Serves 4.*

Almost all the peaches on the market today are freestones—that is, peaches whose pits can be easily removed. Some older peach varieties, which you may find at orchards and farm stands, are clingstones; though delicious for eating whole, they are difficult to use in a recipe calling for halved, pitted fruit.

4 large peaches

2 tablespoons fresh lemon juice

⅓ cup quick-cooking oats

2 tablespoons firmly packed light brown sugar

1 tablespoon finely chopped almonds

1 tablespoon unsalted butter, melted

½ teaspoon cinnamon

Grilled Pears with Butterscotch Sauce

The large broiler grill or a stovetop grill works best with this recipe.

4 large firm-ripe Anjou or
    Bartlett pears

3 tablespoons fresh lime juice

2 tablespoons granulated sugar

⅓ cup evaporated skim milk

2 tablespoons firmly packed
    light brown sugar

2 teaspoons unsalted butter

½ teaspoon vanilla extract

Prepare the grill according to the manufacturer's instructions. Spray the grill with nonstick cooking spray.

Peel the pears, halve them lengthwise, and core. With a sharp knife, cut a very thin slice from the rounded side of each pear half. In a medium bowl, toss the pear halves with the lime juice and granulated sugar.

Grill the pear halves for 4 minutes. Using a spatula, turn the pears and grill for 5 minutes on the stovetop grill, 7 minutes on the broiler grill, or until tender.

Meanwhile, in a small saucepan, combine the evaporated milk, brown sugar, butter, and vanilla. Cook over medium heat, stirring constantly, until the mixture comes to a gentle boil. Cook until the sauce is smooth and slightly thickened, about 2 minutes.

Divide the pears among 4 plates, drizzle with the butterscotch sauce, and serve hot or warm. *Serves 4.*

Grilled Pineapple with Orange-Maple Sauce

The large broiler grill or a stovetop grill works best with this recipe.

1 small pineapple

**¾ cup firmly packed dark
   brown sugar**

3 tablespoons maple syrup

2 tablespoons fresh lime juice

½ teaspoon grated orange zest

⅓ cup fresh orange juice

**2 tablespoons finely chopped
   pecans**

Prepare the grill according to the manufacturer's instructions. Spray the grill with nonstick cooking spray.

Meanwhile, with a large, sharp knife, trim off the top and bottom of the pineapple. Cut the unpeeled pineapple crosswise into 8 rings (each about ¾ inch thick). With an apple corer, sharp knife, or small biscuit cutter, cut the tough center core out of the pineapple rings. In a small skillet, combine the brown sugar, maple syrup, and lime juice. Remove and set aside 2 tablespoons of the mixture.

Grill the pineapple for 6 minutes, turning occasionally, or until golden brown. Brush the pineapple with some of the reserved 2 tablespoons sugar mixture, turn, and grill for 1 minute. Brush with the remaining sugar mixture, turn, and grill for 1 more minute.

Meanwhile, add the orange zest and orange juice to the sugar mixture remaining in the skillet. Bring to a boil over medium heat. Cook until slightly thickened and syrupy, about 4 minutes.

Place the pineapple rings on 4 plates, top with the orange-maple sauce, sprinkle with the pecans, and serve. *Serves 4.*

You can prepare the whole dessert in advance, but don't sprinkle on the nuts until just before serving.

Grilled Bananas with Rum Sauce

Prepare the grill according to the manufacturer's instructions. Spray the grill with nonstick cooking spray.

Grill the bananas for 6 minutes on the broiler grill, 10 to 11 minutes on the stovetop grill, turning occasionally, or until blackened. When cool enough to handle, slit the banana skins with a paring knife and carefully peel off. Cut the bananas on the diagonal into $1/2$-inch slices.

Meanwhile, in a medium saucepan, combine the brown sugar, lime juice, and rum. Bring to a gentle boil over medium heat. Stir in the allspice and nutmeg. Add the sliced bananas to the rum sauce and cook, spooning the sauce over the bananas, until piping hot and well coated, about 3 minutes. Spoon the bananas onto 4 plates and serve. *Serves 4.*

Use bananas that are ripe but still firm, so they don't fall apart when cooked.

4 large bananas (about 8 ounces each), unpeeled
$2/3$ cup firmly packed light brown sugar
$1/2$ cup fresh lime juice
$1/4$ cup dark rum
$1/4$ teaspoon allspice
$1/4$ teaspoon nutmeg

Red Wine and Bay Leaf Marinade

¾ **cup dry red wine**

¼ **cup olive oil**

2 tablespoons red wine vinegar

3 garlic cloves, minced

4 bay leaves

¾ **teaspoon salt**

¼ **teaspoon black pepper**

½ **teaspoon thyme**

In a medium bowl, combine the wine, oil, vinegar, garlic, bay leaves, salt, pepper, and thyme. Marinate meat, covered, in the refrigerator for at least 2 hours or for up to 8 hours. *Serves 6 to 8.*

This marinade adds plenty of flavor to red meat and is especially good on less-expensive cuts, such as chuck steak. For best flavor, cook the meat rare and slice it thin.

White Wine and Rosemary Marinade

I **cup dry white wine**

¾ **cup thinly sliced shallots or onion**

⅓ **cup olive oil**

I **tablespoon plus 2 teaspoons chopped fresh rosemary, or 2 teaspoons dried**

2-inch strip lemon zest

I **tablespoon balsamic vinegar**

2 garlic cloves, lightly crushed

½ **teaspoon salt**

½ **teaspoon black pepper**

In a medium bowl, combine the wine, shallots, oil, rosemary, lemon zest, vinegar, garlic, salt, and pepper. Marinate chicken, veal, or vegetables, covered, in the refrigerator for up to 3 hours. *Serves 6 to 8.*

This recipe makes enough for 2 to 3 pounds chicken, veal, or vegetables.

Lemon-Pepper Marinade

In a small bowl, combine the oil, lemon zest, lemon juice, sugar, pepper, salt, and parsley. Marinate fish, covered, in the refrigerator for 30 minutes; chicken for up to 2 hours. *Serves 6 to 8.*

This recipe makes enough for 1 to 2 pounds of chicken cutlets or fish fillets. Spoon a little of the marinade over the meat a few minutes before it's done for an extra flavor kick.

1/3 **cup olive oil**

1 **tablespoon grated lemon zest**

1/4 **cup plus 2 tablespoons fresh lemon juice**

1 1/2 **teaspoons sugar**

1 1/4 **teaspoons black pepper**

1 **teaspoon salt**

2 **tablespoons chopped parsley**

Pesto Marinade

In a food processor or blender, combine the basil, oil, Parmesan, broth, lemon juice, garlic, pepper, and salt. Purée the mixture for 45 seconds. Marinate meat or poultry, covered, in the refrigerator for 2 hours or overnight; shrimp for up to 1 hour. *Serves 6 to 8.*

More commonly used on pasta, this basil preparation adds punch to grilled chicken (especially skinned thighs), pork cutlets or chops, or shrimp. Don't use all the pesto as a marinade; reserve a little to serve at the table. This recipe makes enough for 2 to 3 pounds meat, poultry, or shrimp.

1 1/2 **cups fresh basil leaves**

3 **tablespoons olive oil**

2 **tablespoons grated Parmesan cheese**

2 **tablespoons chicken broth**

2 **tablespoons fresh lemon juice**

2 **garlic cloves, peeled**

1/4 **teaspoon black pepper**

1/8 **teaspoon salt**

Tomato-Molasses Barbecue Sauce

2 tablespoons unsalted butter

½ **cup chopped onion**

½ **cup diced green bell pepper**

2 garlic cloves, minced

I bay leaf

¼ **teaspoon cloves**

28-ounce can tomatoes, drained
and puréed in food processor

I cup ketchup

6-ounce can tomato paste

¼ **cup cider vinegar**

¼ **cup molasses**

I tablespoon yellow mustard

I teaspoon hot pepper sauce

½ **teaspoon salt**

In a large nonstick saucepan, warm the butter over medium heat until melted. Add the onion, bell pepper, garlic, bay leaf, and cloves and cook, stirring often, until the vegetables are tender, about 5 minutes.

Stir in the tomatoes, ketchup, 1 cup of water, tomato paste, vinegar, molasses, mustard, hot pepper sauce, and salt and bring to a boil. Reduce the heat to low, cover, and simmer, stirring occasionally, until the sauce is thickened, about 40 minutes. Serve hot or cold. *Serves 16.*

This basic sauce is the one everyone is sure to love on ribs, burgers, steaks, chicken, or shrimp. Brush the sauce on only during the last 2 to 3 minutes of grilling, or it will burn. Serve extra sauce at the table for dipping. This recipe makes a big batch but you can halve the recipe, if you prefer. It keeps for weeks in the refrigerator.

Grilled Tomato Salsa

Prepare the grill according to the manufacturer's instructions. Spray the grill with nonstick cooking spray.

On the broiler grill, grill the bell peppers, cut sides down, for 10 minutes, or until charred. On the stovetop grill, grill the bell peppers for 15 to 18 minutes, turning once, or until charred. Meanwhile, grill the jalapeños, cut sides up, for 10 minutes, or until blackened. Remove from the grill and set aside. On the broiler grill, grill the tomatoes, turning once, for 3 to 4 minutes, or until charred. On the stovetop grill, grill the tomatoes, turning on all sides, for 10 minutes, or until charred. Remove from the grill and set aside. Grill the scallions for 2 minutes, or until lightly browned.

Peel the bell peppers. Coarsely chop the bell peppers, jalapeños, and tomatoes and transfer to a large bowl. Slice the scallions and add to the bowl with the cilantro, vinegar, oil, cumin, and salt. Stir until blended. Serve at room temperature. *Serves 4.*

Most of the heat from fresh chili peppers comes from the volatile oils found in the ribs (and to a lesser extent in the seeds). For a tamer dish, omit those parts. When working with chili peppers, fresh or grilled, use rubber gloves to protect your hands and keep your hands away from your face, especially the eyes. Wash your hands thoroughly with hot soapy water when you're done.

2 green bell peppers, halved lengthwise

2 jalapeño peppers, halved lengthwise and seeded

2 pounds medium firm-ripe tomatoes

4 scallions, trimmed

⅓ cup chopped fresh cilantro or parsley

3 tablespoons red wine vinegar

1 teaspoon olive oil

1 teaspoon cumin

1 teaspoon salt

Pineapple–Red Pepper Relish

1 ½ cups finely diced fresh
    pineapple, or drained juice-
    packed canned
1 medium red bell pepper, finely
    diced
2 tablespoons minced red onion
1 tablespoon chopped parsley
2 teaspoons sugar
2 teaspoons red wine vinegar
¼ teaspoon salt
⅛ teaspoon black pepper
⅛ teaspoon red pepper flakes

In a medium bowl, stir together the pineapple, bell pepper, onion, parsley, sugar, vinegar, salt, black pepper, and red pepper flakes until blended. Cover and refrigerate for at least 30 minutes before serving. The relish will keep for 1 to 2 days in the refrigerator. *Serves 8.*

Serve this refreshing and colorful relish alongside grilled chicken or turkey breasts, or with grilled pork cutlets or sea scallops.

Plum-Raisin Chutney

1 tablespoon olive oil
⅓ cup chopped red onion
1 garlic clove, minced
½ teaspoon ground ginger
⅛ teaspoon allspice
3 tablespoons light brown sugar
1 pound fresh plums, diced
⅓ cup golden raisins
2 tablespoons balsamic vinegar

In a medium nonstick saucepan, warm the oil over medium heat. Add the onion, garlic, ginger, and allspice and cook, stirring often, until the onion is tender, 3 to 4 minutes.

Add the sugar and stir until it melts. Stir in the plums and raisins and bring to a simmer. Reduce the heat to medium-low, cover, and simmer, stirring occasionally, until the plums are tender and translucent but not mushy, 5 to 7 minutes.

Add the vinegar and boil, uncovered, for 1 minute. Cover and refrigerate for at least 1 day before serving. The chutney will keep for up to 1 week in the refrigerator. *Serves 8.*

Index

Credits

Food testing and styling:
  Lisa Cherkasky
Recipe editing: Fran Feldman,
  Catherine Boland Hackett
Proofreading: Celia Beattie, April
  Syring

Design: Gibson Parsons Design
Photography: Renée Comet
Photo Assistant: Katherine Dennis Low
Props Coordinator: Kimberly A.
  Grandcolas

Props courtesy of: Appalachian Spring,
April Cornell, Corso De' Fiori, Crate &
Barrel, H.D. Goddin Antiques &
Acanthus Garden, Pier 1 Imports,
Portside, Michael Round, Tamsan
Designs, TJ MAX, and Williams-
Sonoma.

Special thanks to Victoria Kalish,
Jennifer Pearce, and Chris Register.